SUCCESSFUL SKIING

Konrad Bartelski

Illustrations by Alan Batley

Produced in association with

CITROËN U.K. LTD

CITROËN

SACKVILLE
BOOKS

First published in 1989
by Sackville Books Ltd
Stradbroke, Suffolk, England

Deigned and produced by Sackville Design Group Limited
Art Editor: Rolando Ugolini
Editor: Nick Bevan

British Library Cataloguing in Publication Data
Bartelski, Konrad, 1954-
Successful Skiing — (Sackville Sports Clinic Series)
1. Skiing
I. Title
796.93

ISBN 0 948615 30 3

Typeset by Micropress, Halesworth, Suffolk, England.

Reproduction by BPCC Bury Studio, Bury St Edmunds, Suffolk, England

Printed and bound by Proost Internationale Boekproduktie nv, Turnhout,
Belguim

Contents

Konrad Bartelski is one of the most successful British skiers. He took part in three Winter Olympics before he retired in 1983, and in 1981 took second place in the World Cup Downhill Race at Val Gardena: perhaps the best result ever achieved by a British skier. Besides skiing for pleasure and occasionally teaching, he now imports leading ski equipment.

Introduction

Skiing is a sport where, once you've been gripped by its appeal, there is a compelling desire to improve your performance. The beauty of skiing though, is that the enjoyment factor is not directly related to your ability on the slopes. You can have as much fun on the nursery slopes as racing down the icy Hannenkahm World Cup downhill. In fact, beginners are better off, as they spend more time going down the hill, and less time on the lifts! So you don't need to be in a rush to improve!

This book is about some of the basic elements of skiing and I hope will give you a few ideas on how you can take more advantage of the beautiful playground of the mountains.

I believe skiing is really a more straightforward pastime than many people perceive it to be. Looking back over my thirty-one years on snow, I have found that there are many preconceived ideas about skiing which make it a favourite bar-room topic.

Realistically, it is a sport which lends itself much to discussion, but practically, the less effort you spend on the in-depth analysis and the more your spend on the practice, the better results you will have.

The most frustrating aspect about the sport, though, is that more often than not, the reward for grit and determination tends to be a backward step. I have often spent weeks trying to achieve some improvements in my technique, all to no avail. Yet, presented in perhaps less obvious ways later on, this has suddenly resulted in a marked improvement. Most of the time, because I was concentrating on something else, what I was trying to achieve in fact happened automatically.

That is why, if you focus your attention on some of the small points I suggest in this book, I hope you will find that skiing is a bit easier than the last time you tried it.

Whatever you try to do on the slopes though, there is no substitute for a good, solid foundation laid down by spending your learning period in the hands of a good ski instructor.

The most important period for any skier are those first weeks learning the basics, as you find you will always relate to the technique you learnt in the early stages.

But skiing is a bit more than just a sport — this is something you are aware of immediately you get out into the

mountain environment - and for those of us who are fortunate enough to have experienced it, it certainly becomes an aspect of your life with which you want to keep in regular contact.

Although it can absorb your closest attention, it is important to keep a perspective of what it's all about, and to me that is quite simply the basic freedom from all the ritual pressures of our modern-day life.

Although I have completely immersed my life in the sport, I still find that it can provide me with the richest of rewards. I hope too that you will find out that, when it's fun, skiing really is so easy.

I should like to thank Citroën (UK) for assisting me in writing not just another skiing title, but a book that comes from more than thirty years enjoyment in the mountains.

CHAPTER ONE

What is skiing?

You don't have to be a physicist to grasp the basic
principles of skiing — but it does help to think a bit about
what is happening on the mountain to help you to get in
control when you're on it.

The reason you slide down the hill is because gravity is
pulling you down, and the bottom surface of the skis is
designed so that there is relatively little friction between you
and the slippery snow.

*It helps to think a bit about what is happening on the
mountain to help you to stay in control. Gravity is
pulling you down, while the position of your body
counteracts the forces generated by the fact that you
are moving*

Skiing is about controlling gravity so that you can choose your path down the hill, as opposed to going down the hill the way gravity wants you to.

Having said that, the latter does happen occasionally, but then all you have to do is brush off the snow, laugh and try again.

Angulation

All the positions a skier sometimes needs to adopt (and which often feel very awkward) are really the positions the body naturally assumes to adapt to the fact that they are moving downhill with gravity, and to absorb the changes in terrain.

Angulation in a turn, or while traversing, is one of the most awkward positions an instructor demands — or a skier fights to achieve. Really, all the teacher is asking their pupil to do is to let their body compensate for the effects of gravity on itself while moving. This will appear in the form of the body bending sideways at the waist — which is what skiers call angulation. What you are doing is bringing the weight of your body over the ski that needs the pressure on it in order to execute the turn or to be stable on a traverse.

If you can grasp this and feel that you are controlling the basic principle using the basic tools your body has (as opposed to forcing your skis down the hill), you will find it easier to relax on your skis.

Ski design

Skis are designed to help you control the forces of gravity over different types of terrain, at varying speeds and over the very different surfaces, such as packed snow found on the piste, or the more scary ice. Skis in good condition make this easier for you.

If you were to jump off your skis while traversing, they would automatically point straight down the hill. If, then, you jumped back on the skis and directed a little bit of weight on the inside of the right ski, they would then turn to the left. The more of your body-weight you allowed to come down on to the ski, the sharper the turn would be.

This point about the weight being on and off the ski is the pivotal point of skiing. This is how you use your instruments, the skis, to control the gravity which is pulling you down.

The weighting/unweighting motion is important whether you are a novice or a champion. Watch any World Cup race on television and you will see the competitor allows all their energy onto the ski on the outside of each turn. In betweeen turns they seem to float, as they are "unweighted"

In a snowplough turn, as you lean over the ski you want to turn, you are 'weighting' the ski, so it turns. Then, when the turn is completed, you naturally get the weight back on to both of the skis, so half of your weight is on each ski. This means you are putting less weight on the turning ski than you did in the turn, so that the ski has had weight taken off it — you have automatically unweighted the ski.

Watch any racer in a World Cup race, and you'll see that he has all his weight over the lower ski through the turn, but at the end of the turn he is nearly standing straight up on his skis. This is because his full body-weight, increased by the centrifugal force, has been over the turning ski, but at the end of the turn he does not want any weight on his skis. Therefore he extends his legs to take the weight of his upper body off the skis. That is the same weighting/unweighting motion that a snowplough skier experiences.

Allowing your senses to feel this happening — particularly when you are learning — and trying to understand why it is working for you — will help you progress quickly.

CHAPTER TWO

Skiing — it's easy

When you first step out on a pair of skis, be it on beautiful, snow-covered mountain slopes, or even on one of the numerous dry slopes around Britain, the most important thing to remember — and surprisingly many people forget this — is that being on skis is a way like no other to enjoy yourself!

Many a skier has clenched their fists on their first journey to the mountains and vowed to make startling progress down the slopes, under the misapprehension that the faster you travel, the more pleasure you will have.

Those skiers have got it wrong before they have even taken up the sport. Learning to ski can be one of the most memorable experiences. There is no point rushing through the basics, because if you do not master the essential tools of the trade, you will not have the reserves to fall back on (hopefully not literally) when you are in a tricky situation. So, if you are patient when you start off, and resist the temptation to try to do too much too quickly, you will find that all the pieces of the jigsaw puzzle will fall easily into place.

Look out for number one

When you are standing on those fearsome planks, which threaten to whisk you away down the hill, and you look around the nursery slopes, there are always lot of little kids which hardly come up to your knees, racing down the snow. There's no doubt, it's terribly demoralizing to watch these fearless tots darting about the slopes with so much energy and enthusiasm.

The first rule of learning to ski is to think only about yourself. Do not worry about what anybody else is thinking about your performance — the other skiers are all concentrating on what they are doing, and they've probably got their hands full just staying standing up as well! You don't need to compare your progress with that of other people in the class, or your husband, wife or friends — it's not really relevant to how much you enjoy yourself. When you start to worry about not progressing fast enough or you feel that people might take the view that you are not very competent, then your problems will start. Your muscles will strain that bit more, your legs will start forcing the skis around - and basically your timing will go out the window. All that will happen is that you will end of up more tired, frustrated and fed up — not really what a holiday is for!

Skiing is a very psychological sport, and if you tackle it as a way to have fun, your body will naturally find the best positions to be in. This is a more relaxing way of approaching what can be a tiring sport, especially if you go all out for muscles and determination. You'll find the learning process is noticeably quicker if you relax.

The first rule of learning to ski is to think about yourself. Do not worry about what anybody else might be thinking about your efforts — the others skiers probably have their hands full already!

CHAPTER THREE

Exploring your senses

Your body has millions of nerves which allow you to feel what is happening around you. Make use of the messages which these sensitive areas around the body report to your brain about the changes which are happening around you as you move down the hill.

Try to feel where your arms and legs are — but don't try to force your limbs into positions, as that will make your muscles tight. So, before you head off from the top of the mountain, just look around you — enjoy the scenery and then consciously feel where each foot and hand is. That way, when you issue instructions to your limbs, you know where the message is going. Similarly, if you keep this line of communication open, you will be able to translate the messages being received from these important receptors on your way down.

It is important to FEEL what you are doing, as this improves your co-ordination — and this allows your body to respond naturally. If, on the other hand, you try to force or push your body into positions, the tightening of your muscles interferes with the commands from the control tower — your head.

This is why, when skiers get on to slopes that they feel are too steep, and suddenly generate a certain amount of nervous anticipation, they suddenly find themselves in more trouble than the situation warrants.

What happens is that the body tenses and blocks the path which the normal commands travel along. If you try to ignore the psychological aspect of the steep slope below you and breathe deeply to relax your body, your co-ordination will miraculously return.

It is best to feel for yourself how your body is reacting to this new, seemingly hostile environment. For example, if you feel confident on the easier slopes — you might be practising a lot of different exercises well — then you might want to take on new challenges on more difficult terrain. If you have not fully built up your confidence in the basic requirements for the standard of terrain you want to tackle — stopping turning and traversing — you will tense up, often just sub-consciously, at the sight of the new, more challenging slopes. Suddenly you will think that you are struggling to do what you want to, because the tension is

Before you slide off — stop and consciously feel where each hand and foot is. Then when you "issue instructions" to your limbs, you have a better "feel" of what is happening

blocking the free passage of messages to and from your limbs. This is when you stop feeling what is happening and probably feel just what is not happening!

Try to control this by getting a feel for what parts of the mountain you are comfortable on, because if you build up good, strong confidence before you tackle more difficult slopes, you will handle the tougher challenges a lot more easily.

Quite simply, if you feel good, your skiing will be good — so remember to feel what is happening.

Feeling through your feet

Even when you are flying over an icy downhill course at 85 mph, you can still feel exactly what is happening underneath you through the soles of your feet. Ski racers like to have ski boots that are as thin as possible, so that their feet can be sensitive to the snow. This is because the soles of a skier's feet are like a blind man's fingers reading Braille. Their vision is directed ahead in anticipation of what is coming up, while their feet are continuously reading what is happening at the time. When you are skiing a good race, the feeling is so subtle and precise that you can almost feel the snow flakes you are flying over. A good racer is not necessarily the one who uses all their brute force to fight their way down the hill, but the one who is sensitive to the slope and uses the least amount of force to achieve the necessary changes in direction.

It is the same when YOU are skiing. If you can feel for yourself how little movement and muscle power is necessary to go down the hill, you will be surprised at what you can achieve.

Try to do as little as possible on the way down a slope, making sure that what you do is correct — and you will probably float down the hill quite effortlessly. You'll have more control too — all because you are trying to feel what is happening to the ground under your feet.

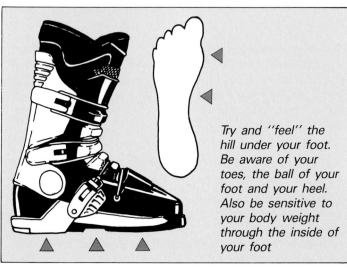

Try and "feel" the hill under your foot. Be aware of your toes, the ball of your foot and your heel. Also be sensitive to your body weight through the inside of your foot

CHAPTER FOUR

The mountain — its potential and limitations

To get the most out of your winter holiday, especially your first one, it's worth spending a little time trying to understand a bit about this new and very alien environment.

It's not just the obvious points of being aware of the hazards to look out for — it's being in a position to take advantage of what these beautiful mountains have to offer you.

It never fails to amaze me when I am skiing with a group of holiday-makers and we all stop to regroup, that after a few minutes, when I point out the view, there is a sudden rush to grab the cameras, even though they have been standing there for a few minutes getting their breath back.

It is important to absorb the scenery and to take in the subtle changes as you move around the countryside. Even when it's snowing heavily in cold weather, you can enjoy studying the fine crystals as they land on your legs when you are going up the chair lift, or spot the marmots scurrying around their snow-holes. The wildlife leaves interesting marks around freshly fallen snow, and identifying their prints can add a touch of the David Attenboroughs to a long chair-lift ride.

As you find yourself taking more interest in what's going on in the mountains, try applying the same adventurous approach to the way you ski down a mountain.

Obviously you can explore the different runs suitable to your ability and organise trips around the resort to check out the different mountain restaurants, but on each of the marked runs, you should explore the natural terrain and 'feel' the changes of the slope beneath you. Let the gentle rolls of a broad, open piste unweight the skis for you, use the full width of the well groomed slopes to make some large, smooth turns and use your eyes to pick out the best areas on the slope.

Frequently it's not better technique that makes a skier more proficient, but their expertise in making the best of the numerous options open to them.

Once you develop that awareness in the mountains, you can really speed up the learning process. A good ski instructor who enjoys his teaching and loves the mountains will automatically inspire their pupils with the wisdom which

▲

It is important to absorb the scenery and take in the beautiful countryside.

◀

Explore the natural terrain and "feel" the changes of the slope beneath you.

he has built up over many years, but you can improve your own ability to absorb the surroundings by just stopping occasionally and taking time to see what is around you.

As you start to ski faster, this naturally becomes even more important, as you need to keep an eye on any potential obstacles, and watch for other less expert skiers on the slopes. Before setting off, you should identify any possible hazards, just as an aircraft pilot plots his flight. A bit of thought at the right time makes it so much easier to ski in control and to enjoy yourself.

CHAPTER FIVE

Back to basics

To progress in your skiing in an attempt to reach a new level, you naturally TRY to grit your teeth, inject some extra determination into your efforts and wait for that magic progression to occur.

You'll usually wind up with a few tired muscles, and possibly some spare words, not normally found in the dictionary. More often than not, that extra effort you are putting in to find that strived-for extra form will tend to tense your body up and upset your timing to such an extent that everything you have learnt up to that point will be lost—swamped by your new-found aggression.

To get off the plateau that you find yourself on, where you seem to be stuck and not progressing any further, try taking some time and going back to the beginning.

Developing control

The foundation of all your skiing skills are those exercises which you performed on the nursery slopes. Go back to a nice open slope and practise the easiest of manoeuvres —the snowplough stop.

Always give yourself a target at which to stop, and try to get perfectly accurate, so that your ski tips stop exactly at the mark in the snow that you have chosen. When you have mastered this — and you will probably surprise yourself by finding out that it will take you a few tries to get it exactly correct — then do the same, but this time on a steeper slope.

Make sure you adopt a comfortable, relaxed position, with your hands just in the lower corner of your vision, before you start off. Then get some speed up and make a good, clean positive stop, exactly at the predetermined mark.

When you've got this exercise nailed, go back to the more gentle slope again and do the basic snowploughs, linking them neatly together, trying to be as smooth and fluid as possible. Slowly build up a good rhythm, until you transfer the weight easily from the one outside ski in the turn to the other outside ski. Feel all the time how the change in the weight on the skis translates into changes of direction.

Exaggerate the movements of your legs and experiment by

Develop your control by putting your hat or a marker in the snow and stopping just in front of it.

radical unweighting of the skis. Play around a bit and find out what differences you can conjure up by doing what may seem like daft exercises on these easy slopes, where you naturally feel almost over-confident.

Learning by experiment

Try doing things differently from the way you normally do them and just see what happens. You will quickly get reports from your body and/or your skis if the experiments are not helping, but by trying different things on such an easy slope, you should be able to receive a lot of messages from your feet and skis about the effect they can have on

Practise with basic linked, snowplough turns on a gentle slope. Slowly build up a good rhythm, until you transfer the weight easily from one outside ski in the turn to the other. Exaggerate the movements of your legs and experiment by more radical unweighting of the skis. Play around a bit and find out what differences you can conjure up, by doing what may seem like daft movements on these easy slopes

your skiing. Suddenly you might notice that things you felt you needed masses of force and energy to execute, can almost happen by themselves — on the other hand, you might find out that the way you were doing it was, for you, the most economical way of skiing. Whichever you discover, at least you will have found out for yourself the basic positions in which you feel the most comfortable.

So, now you have settled yourself down on the easy slopes, and have subconsciously regained a bit more confidence, then it's time to head back up the mountains and try the areas that you felt were giving you problems before. You'll surprise yourself — if you have practised diligently what seemed almost too easy — by how suddenly the more difficult parts of the slope slide by that bit more gently.

If you are starting off your holiday, after you have got over the initial excitement of being back in the beautiful winter world, take a few minutes to 'go back to basics'. You will notice that you find your ski-legs just that much more quickly.

CHAPTER SIX

Know your limits

While you need to understand the mountains and the
environment in which you ski, it is just as important to know
your own limitations. Skiing is a very deceptive sport, in that
even when you watch Franz Klammer rattling down the
Lauberhorn in Wengen, you do not really get the impression
that he is working all that hard — not in the same way
Steve Cram might at the end of an 800 metres race.

In fact, his legs will be burning, in spite of the intense,
year-round training programme that puts his physical fitness
on a par with any world-class athlete. Similarly, when you
are sliding down, even the easy slopes, the effort you are
putting in is certainly a lot more than most people put in
during their normal lives.

You must accept that skiing is hard work and understand
that you cannot initially achieve everything that you want to
on the first day. You will find that, by taking it easier and
controlling your enthusiasm, you will end up much further
along the road to achieving your aims.

First day back

On the first day it is so easy to try to start where you left
off the last time you were on the pistes. You've got the
excitement of being back on holiday in the mountains, and
the feeling that you could ski until midnight, if the sun would
only stay up. Unfortunately, it is probably more than eleven
months since you were last on skis, and perhaps you don't
remember the next day, when you lifted your legs out of
bed in the morning — and nothing happened.

It then takes a few days, often uncomfortable ones too,
before the rust works its way out of your system, and the
flexibility returns to your tortured body. By then you might
have missed half of your holiday. You probably find, when
the ski instructor asks you to relax and be flexible, that all
you can think about are the rods of iron welded into the
backs of your legs. No wonder you can't make any
progress.

On the first day, don't try to break any records. Enjoy
your lunch, and have a second coffee or a fresh hot
chocolate — and stop on the early side. Don't go for that

extra run, even though you want to. It will still be there when you go back out tomorrow, and you will be fresher and fitter to enjoy the run even more.

Similarly, when you are tackling different runs from the tops of the mountains, try to choose runs that are within your capabilities, so that you feel that it's no problem to relax on your skis. Occasionally you might find yourself on a stretch of slope that is steeper than what you are used to. If this is the case, be patient and take your time to get through the difficult section. If you feel that you are holding someone back, if they cannot wait for you as you tackle the challenge — then they are not worth the extra energy that you are exerting to try to keep up! Skiing is a sport which everyone has the right to enjoy in their own time, and you have as much right as anyone to be selfish — it's in your own interest!

How competent are you?

If, during your holiday, you try to understand your competence on skis, it makes it easier to select both your next year's destination (there is little point in going to a resort that does not have many suitable runs, when the selection of resorts is so vast), and the correct equipment for your ability. It helps if you have skis which will turn easily for you, but still give you that comforting grip on slippery ice. Both are major contributory factors in making your holiday a good one.

Skiers are split into three internationally recognized general categories for selecting equipment — S, A and L.

S skiers
This denotes the standard of a sporty, recreational skier, who is quite a fast, competent skier on black runs. Within this category there are skiers who prefer the bumpy mogul slopes and those who prefer the open, prepared pistes, while the fresh powder snow remains the ultimate attraction for others. Speed is of the essence, normally for the younger skiers, while perfection of style is the main aim of many skiers in this group.

A skiers
This standard applies to the recreational skier who has progressed away from the snowplough turn and is confident and relaxed on red runs. Most skiers fall into this category,

and it covers a broad spectrum of ability. Some people like to go fast — others meander gently down the slope, while others are perfecting their parallel turns — not yet venturing on to the steeper pistes. If you are trying to define your ability in this area, you must try to take into account the speed with which you are progressing, and your ambitions on the slopes. If you want to be able to fly through the mogul slopes by the end of the next holiday, then your requirements are very different from those of someone who just wants to explore the variety of a large ski resort.

L skiers

These are the skiers who are learning the basics of snowploughing and beyond. An 'L' skier will spend most of their time on the blue runs, occasionally breaking out of the snowplough into basic stem turns, but capable of getting themselves around the easy runs.

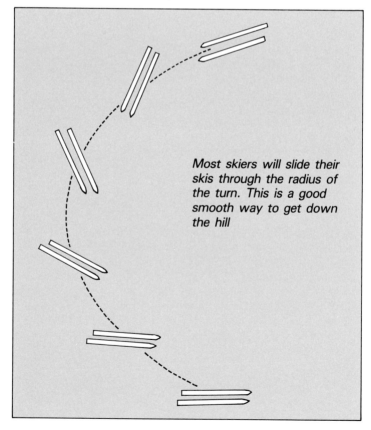

Most skiers will slide their skis through the radius of the turn. This is a good smooth way to get down the hill

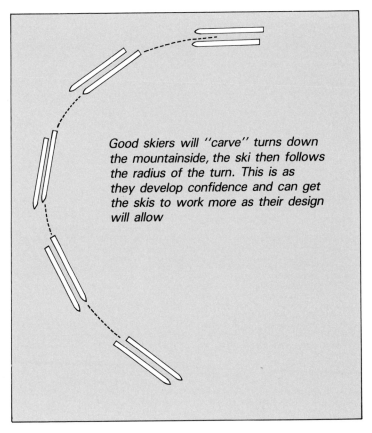

Good skiers will "carve" turns down the mountainside, the ski then follows the radius of the turn. This is as they develop confidence and can get the skis to work more as their design will allow

If you have grasped a picture of your requirements within these areas, this will help, for example, if you join up with a new class in ski school. Not only that, if you try to understand what your level of skiing is, it is then easier to set out realistically obtainable targets to aim for on your holiday.

Don't be embarrassed if you place relatively little importance on making massive progress — if you are happy with your level of skiing and feel that you can ski well enough to enjoy yourself, then that's all you need to do to have a good holiday. After all, that's what it's all about!

CHAPTER SEVEN

To go, stop

When you are skiing, you will have nothing to worry about if you can stop. If you can stop confidently, you will always be in control — and if you feel you are in control, you will relax and progress faster.

The basic tool for stopping is the snowplough. It is amazing that even some expert skiers forget the essential basic control you need to stop in this position.

The basic snowplough is the safe platform from which all your skiing can develop. If you ask an expert skier to make a few snowplough turns, they will almost certainly make the same mistakes that they would make when skiing at their usual speed.

Snowplough practice

To master the snowplough, you need to choose an open, gentle slope. By practising on this easy slope you can develop your feeling for your skis and establish a better understanding of what those slippery boards can do for you.

Women start off with a slight natural advantage in performing this manoeuvre, as their physical make-up is more suited to the exercise. Their hips tend to be wider, while their legs are slightly knock-kneed - a physical build which automatically brings the weight correctly on the inside edges of the skis (the inside edges being the bottom of the sides of the skis which face each other when you are standing on them). The male body structure, with narrower hips and a tendency towards being bow-legged, makes the snowplough a less natural posture, while children infuriatingly seem to take up this position quite naturally.

To start practising the snowplough, find a nice flat spot and point your skis in the direction down the slope of the hill. Stand comfortably on your skis, with your feet apart to about the width of your hips. Let your hands drop down loosely and, while you are looking straight ahead, bring them both up slowly until you can just see them in the bottom of your vision. You should feel as if you could drive the number 42 bus down the road. Just relax in this position — naturally you can only do this if the area around you is flat.

Gently push — or step — the heels of your skis out, so

that the tails are wide apart. Rest the weight of your body, through your legs, on the inside of the skis. Once your skis are apart, don't push down hard on the skis — your body, from the waist up, provides enough weight or pressure to control the skis. Your muscles do not really need to press or push any more. Your legs direct your upper body and allow this weight to come over the skis in the right place, so giving you control of them. The exact width the skis are apart is not important, as long as you feel comfortable, and you feel you could always push them wider apart if

The basic snowplough is the safe platform from which all skiing can develop. Practise this manoeuvre on easy terrain until you feel comfortable and can stop well

Even if you have skied a lot, a few minutes practising the snowplough stop on your first day will help you get your "feeling" and timing back

necessary. Relax in this position — look up around you and enjoy the view. Now push yourself forward gently using your two ski poles — you should slide forward towards the slope. As you start to slide down the slope, rock backwards and forward gently until you find the most comfortable position, still keeping your weight equally on both skis. This should be your ideal snowplough.

Stopping targets

Choose yourself a spot on the snow and let the tails of your skis slide out wider, by gently pushing your feet apart through the heels — you will slow down. Now try to stop at your selected spot. Practise this braking a few times until you are in control of your speed and can stop exactly where you want every time. Even if you have skied a lot of times, a few minutes practising this manoeuvre will help you get your 'feeling' and timing back.

One common problem you may encounter in this position is that your ski tips cross. That is because you are trying too hard and you are pushing your knees together too much. Just relax your legs and be a bit more patient. You will find that you will slow down as soon as your tails get wider apart.

When you can regulate your speed effectively, you will gain confidence. Now is the time to practise changing the width of the snowplough by letting your knees flex, or bend further forward, pointing them slightly to the inside of your ski tips. Feel what happens when you make these changes. You will notice your speed down the slopes changes with your movements. Try to find a longer slope so that you can get some rhythm into this exercise, so that you end up almost bouncing up and down into a narrower and then a wider plough position. From these basic manoeuvres you can evolve all your steps in skiing — even when you are flying over the Kitzbuhel downhill at 80 mph!

CHAPTER EIGHT

Snowplough turns — building the foundation

Snow plough turns are most probably the way in which you will make your first deliberate changes of direction.

When you feel comfortable using the basic snowplough to stop, it is amazing how easy it is to change this into a turning manoeuvre. The basics which you learn at this very early stage carry right through to racing level. The same fast turns that you see Ingemar Stenmark performing down an icy slope are really an extension of the basics learnt, most probably, on your first day on skis.

Using your weight

If you feel you can control stopping, then you will almost certainly be surprised how easy it is to make your skis go the way you want them to. Try sliding straight down the slope and simply put more weight on one ski than the other. Don't try to push the ski down, but lean easily just a little bit more to one side. The ski that you are leaning over will come round and turn under you. Lean to the left and you will go to the right, and vice versa. It really is that easy!

When you can master these changes of direction and can link a number of changes of direction together, you can move on to the next step. To turn more and get better control in the radius of the turn, do the same as before, but this time make a definite point of trying to 'stand still' between the turns before you bring you weight back on to the ski that you want to turn. When you bring your weight on to the ski, let your leg bend a bit. Bend it more, and for longer, if you want to turn more, and make a quicker movement if you want a shorter turn.

Experiment for yourself, with different pressure on the skis and different speed in your movements. This way you can feel for yourself what is happening. It is so much easier to understand if you can FEEL the way different movements can influence what is happening to you as you slide down the slope.

Don't forget, though, that the more relaxed you are now, the more you will feel what is happening. That means you will be enjoying yourself more — and therefore you will progress even faster.

Don't try and push
your skis around the
slope, but gently
change the pressure
on your skis by
moving your body
over the ski you
want to turn

Once you have got
your skis to turn,
gently move your
body back through
the normal
snowplough position
so that your body
weight comes onto
the opposite ski, you
will then turn the
other way

When you have the feel of turning, try to make a more distinctive move as you start the turn by letting your leg bend more. Your knee will go forward and your body still will come over the ski you want to turn.

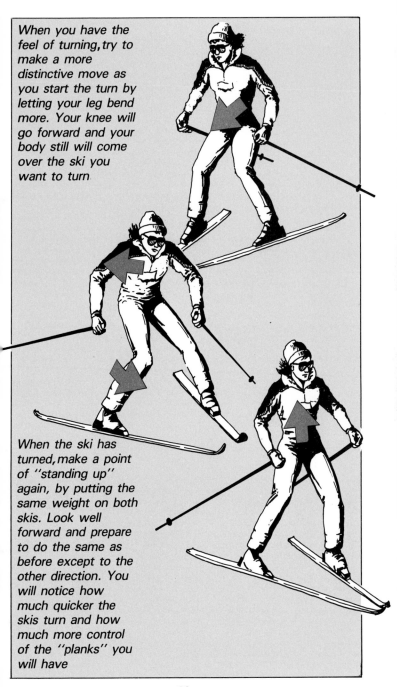

When the ski has turned, make a point of "standing up" again, by putting the same weight on both skis. Look well forward and prepare to do the same as before except to the other direction. You will notice how much quicker the skis turn and how much more control of the "planks" you will have

If you feel, at this stage, that the basic turns are not working out well, go back and practise the snowplough stops for a spell to get the right feeling back.

Stay flexible

To help you progress further, stop for a while as you are practising. Find a nice flat spot and stand in the same position as you did when you started off. Stand quite straight and reach down sideways with your hand, without bending forward, to your knees. Feel the flexibility in your waist. It's important to maintain this when you are skiing — try to use this flexibility in your waist to get your upper body over the skis in the turn. This will allow you to use your own body-weight more effectively, without having to push your skis round the turn. That is the key to easy skiing.

To feel flexibility in your waist, stand in a traverse position and bend down with your downhill hand, touch your knee and relax for a minute. Just make sure you are still looking in the direction you will be travelling

CHAPTER NINE

Traversing and sideslipping

Traversing is the means by which you can go across the hill without sliding down and, along with stopping, it is one of the key pieces of the skiing jigsaw puzzle.

This is probably what most learners of the sport find the most awkward transition, yet it is the position which CAN come most naturally — if you let it! Imagine that someone is trying to pull you down the hill by your lower pole and you are trying to resist it. You automatically adopt an excellent traverse position. So, before you start traversing, bear in mind that you CAN do it

The traverse position is what most people find the most awkward, yet it is the position that CAN come most naturally — if you let it!

The right stance

The key to feeling comfortable when you are standing with your skis sideways across the hill, is to keep most of your weight on the bottom ski (that being the ski closest to the bottom of the hill). Direct this weight over the inside edge of your lower ski, by moving your knee over the inside of your ski boot. It sounds complicated, but really all you are doing is the same as if you were climbing sideways up a hill in your shoes — in other words, digging in. You try to keep the soles of your shoe horizontal to the slope so that you feel the inside of your lower leg gripping on the grass.

Stand in this position, let your knees flex slightly forward and relax. Now lift your head up and look forward, and then down the hill in the direction in which you are going to travel.

If you keep your hands just in view when you have turned your head slightly, your might just find yourself in the correct position! You should feel as if you could be sitting sideways on a fence.

Take your hand which is highest up the hill and reach over to the outside of your lower knee. If you find this easy, then you are standing well over your skis. If it is difficult, then slide your higher foot forward a little and take nearly all your weight off it while you reach round. If you are still finding it difficult, this is because you are not feeling in control and are too tense. The best way to progress is to spend another afternoon practising your snowploughs.

Traversing

Before you begin to move, it is important to feel that you have control of your speed in this manoeuvre by varying the extent to which your skis point downhill. If they are pointing straight across the hill, you will stop. Point the tips a little bit down the hill and you will gradually slide forwards. Point them further down the hill, and you will accelerate more quickly.

If you push off with your poles and slide smoothly across the hill, you will find that you stay in control as long as your weight is over your lower ski and you are looking well down the hill. This is important, as it helps you to see where you

If you are in a traverse or exiting a turn, to remember the correct position, just think that you should be sitting on the side of a fence

are going—or might be going. If the slope gets steeper, adjust by allowing your lower knee to come over the inside of the boot more. You will find that you will have to 'sit more sideways on the fence' to keep that weight on the lower ski.

Try doing this both to the right and left across the hill, aiming for a spot each time so that you feel that you can control your direction. If it is warm, use your hat as a marker.

Always be patient and never try to rush through this exercise. Start off when you are feeling comfortable and breathe out as you are sliding across the hill.

If you feel that you are sliding away down the hill, look to see where you might slide to. You will probably find you simultaneously stop sliding that way.

When you feel comfortable doing this over slightly bumpier terrain, try lifting your inside ski to get good control and balance on just the one ski. Don't forget to do this exercise both to the left and the right.

To sideslip, just walk sideways down from your traverse position. When you move your lower leg down the hill, plant your poles for support. Then as you bring your upper leg to join your lower leg, relax and you will slide

To master this exercise properly, bounce up and down gently while keeping one ski a few inches in the air. Your lower leg should always be flexible, not taut or tense.

Sideslipping

Sideslipping allows you to control the way you cross the slope. It also helps to teach you the 'feel' of the skis sliding sideways down the slope, and is a helpful way to control your speed on steeper terrain.

You will feel that you can reduce the amount of grip of your skis on the slope by carefully letting your knees rock sideways. The more the knees rock down the slope, the more the skis will slide

Moving slowly along in a traverse, just let your body weight come down on the skis by bending your knees forward suddenly, at the same time directing your knees slightly down the hill from the direction of your ski tips.

There are different ways to start to sideslip, but for all of them you should start in the traverse position. You could then step downhill, which is like walking sideways down a staircase.

You can also reduce the amount of grip which your edges have on the snow by directing your knees laterally downhill by just a small amount. By varying the amount you let your knees rock sideways, you will vary your speed down the slope.

Alternatively, moving along a traverse, just let your body-weight come down on to the skis by bending your knees forward strongly, at the same time directing your knees slightly down the hill from the direction of your ski tips.

Now you can cross the slopes, control your speed going downhill and turn to avoid obstacles. Those are all the basic requirements that you need to be able to enjoy the mountains and all the secrets hidden higher up those glistening white peaks. You can ski!

CHAPTER TEN

Learning — getting the best from your instructor

If you have never skied before, I would always recommend making sure your very first steps on snow are with a recognized ski instructor. Your first days on snow provide the basic foundation from which all your future skiing develops.

Once you feel competent on your skis, skiing with a good instructor can only improve your ability, as well as your knowledge of the resort and its interesting features — not to mention some of the local gossip as well.

It is often a good idea to spend the first few days back on skis enjoying some expert tuition too, as the instructor will pace you through your comeback and make sure you start off again on the right foot.

Teaching styles

The style of tuition you are likely to receive depends very much on the country in which you are learning to ski. I learned to ski in Kitzbuhel, Austria, and I owe a lot to the patience of my charming instructress. It was certainly a high spot for me, eight years later, to charge down the Hannenkahm downhill course with my former ski instructor watching at the finish.

The Austrians tend to spend a little less time than others concentrating just on the technique — they prefer to place the emphasis on enjoying the *gemütlichkeit* (atmosphere) of the mountains, cleverly blending the pleasure of being in an alpine environment with the occasional work you need to throw in to keep the skiing going in the right direction.

On the other extreme, the French tend to be more serious and technical — if you can understand them. Somehow they do not seem to have the same pride about seeing their pupils improve as some other nations do, and this is further compounded by their frequent inability to attempt even the most basic rudiments of their tourists' language.

In between these two the Swiss, Germans and Italians add their own national flavour to their teaching methods, while in either Andorra or Scotland you will always find a host of well schooled, experienced and dedicated British ski teachers with that vital sense of humour.

Making the best of tuition

To get the best out of ski school, you should always be realistic in assessing your own ability when you ask to be put in a class. It is always better to start off with a class that is slightly on the slow side than to spend your first days on skis forever catching your breath. It's easier to move up a class after a day or two, and you will automatically feel better than if you have to be put down a class early on.

More often than not, if you are on holiday with a friend, you'll try to keep together in a class — but ideally you ought to make sure the class is, first and foremost, the right one for your ability. If your friend is going to a higher or lower class, you can always arrange to meet them for tea in the afternoon. It really is far better if you can progress at your own pace. It's remarkable (and this is one of the pleasures of a skiing holiday) how quickly you will find friends among a group of strangers, often from completely different backgrounds.

If you have a good teacher, he will insure that the pupil following him changes frequently. That is because the best place to be in the class is immediately behind the teacher. This way you can follow exactly where they go, and how they go about it — after all, imitation is one of the best ways of learning on skis.

All the same, don't hog the prime spot — it's only fair that everyone in the class should have a chance to hold the best position, so that the whole class can progress at the same rate.

Class communication

Always listen carefully when the instructor explains what to do. Sometimes you might have a bit of difficulty in hearing each word due to a broken accent, or to the wind carrying away the words. If that is the case, just ask the instructor to repeat what he said. It's always much better and safer if you understand what he is trying to get across.

If you find that you are not getting on well with your particular teacher, see the Ski School Head at the end of the day and ask if you can move into another class. It is important that you establish a good line of communication, because your teacher must be able to understand what you find difficult and why. He can only do this if you can both get the message across reasonably well — sign language included.

Skiing sense in a class

Never ski on the tails of the pupil in front of you — leave a bit of space, but try to follow the path of the class, as your instructor will always try to find the parts of the slope which are most suitable for your standard.

If you feel your are getting tired, don't hesitate to suggest a pitstop — most probably everyone else in the class is suffering as well, but they are just too shy or too proud to ask for themselves. Similarly, if you feel that all the extra exercise is catching up with you after a few days, perhaps take an afternoon off after lunch and visit the local swimming pool or sauna to give your aching muscles a bit of a break. When I was racing, a day off was as important to

Make sure you can understand or hear clearly what the ski instructor is asking you to do. If you do not understand what he means, then ask him to explain it again. Do not be afraid to speak up, after all it is your holiday.

our training schedule as a day's training.

While your are in the early phases of your skiing, you will almost certainly benefit from returning to the same resort for a few years. The slopes will be familiar, so you won't be intimidated by the unknown, and you will get to know the ski school well — a factor which can only help you to learn more quickly and easily.

When you feel that you are more accomplished on the planks, then you are in a better position to be adventurous. Often your instructor may ask you to do something you find extremely awkward and difficult as you ski down. If this is the case, stop for a breather, enjoy the scenery, shake out your arms and legs, take a deep breath and try again. If you still find the exercise difficult, ask the instructor to explain again, either because you don't understand what he means, or because you cannot do it. Bear in mind that, if you don't say anything, your instructor will think you are happy with the way things are going. Don't be afraid to speak up — after all, it is your holiday.

CHAPTER ELEVEN

Key tips

When you first jump on your skis, there are so many things to think about. It's quite difficult to remember everything you might need to do — so much so that you can get quite confused, especially if you want to spend some time improving your skiing. The following key tips are easy-to-remember tricks, with which to experiment for a while each day — try concentrating on one of the following at a time and see yourself improve!

Breathing

The most obvious subconscious natural reaction you have is the way you recharge your oxygen level — that is, until you put on your skis.

Breathe deeply out, pushing the air out of the bottom of your lungs, at the end of each turn

Skiing is a physically demanding sport — your muscles have to work hard — but all too frequently you only realize this the next day when you try to get out of bed!

As it is so physical, it's important to replenish all the energy you are expending by taking in plenty of fresh oxygen — which is also in shorter supply at altitude in the mountains.

Remember to breathe out deeply just before you push off down the mountain, and then breathe out deeply after each turn to rid the lungs of all that stale carbon-dioxide. You will automatically refill your lungs with fresh oxygen and you will quickly notice that you can ski further down the hillside without stopping.

Although you might not notice it, the best by-product of your good breathing will be marked improvements in your technique. As you exhale, your upper body has to be relaxed and naturally your legs will do the majority of the work — something your teacher is telling you to do all the time! Being relaxed between turns means that you will find your timing for making each turn a lot more easily. So do the obvious — breathe properly the next time you go skiing!

Pole planting

Always think of your ski pole as a conductor would regard his baton. Ski poles are too often simply regarded as objects which are a nuisance to carry around — but if you watch any good skier, you will notice that they use their ski poles for every turn they make. This also applies to the world's best ski racers as well.

Planting the pole is really important for making a good turn because, when you plant the pole just ahead of you in the snow, you will automatically initiate the weighting of the ski.

As you turn around the pole in the snow, you should naturally unweight. The pole planting reinforces this process which is the easiest way to get your skis to turn, as well as co-ordinating the timing of the manoeuvre.

To use your poles well, always have them where you need them — just at hand, as if you were driving a bus. Make sure you keep them there too — after all, why waste energy by bringing them back from alongside your body (a very common fault). It is more economical to use the action of your wrist to plant the pole than to use your whole arm. That way, your arms are less likely to upset the rest of your

Speed is a word that instils fear in a lot of skiers, but in fact, used correctly, it can not only make your skiing easier, but also more enjoyable

Ski poles are too often simply regarded as objects which are a nuisance to carry around — but watch any good skier, they use their poles for every turn they make

upper body, which should really be as straight as possible, relative to your direction of travel.

Speed

Speed is a word which instils fear in a lot of skiers, but in fact, used correctly, it can not only make your skiing easier, but also more enjoyable.

One of the common problems you encounter on steeper slopes is that the turning suddenly becomes very difficult. This is because you traverse across the mountain and worry about being able to turn on such a difficult gradient — so much so that when you come to make the turn, you are so cautious you almost stop. If you are only travelling slowly, it is very difficult to unweight the skis without jumping around erratically — you need a bit of momentum to help you.

If you are on flatter slopes you can use your speed to make improvements in your skiing, as the skis react more

When you first venture off the nursery slopes, notice how the mountain is changing all the time. Use the changes in terrain to your advantage

easily to your commands. So, concentrate on having a bit of speed when you make a turn, as opposed to slowing down too much. The reasoning works in reverse too — you'll notice that turning is in itself a good way to control your speed.

Using the terrain

When you venture off the nursery slopes, the first most noticeable thing is the way the mountain is changing all the time. Even large, well groomed pistes have long, gentle rolls which meander down the hillside. Often, when you venture out on to these slopes, you don't take advantage of what the mountain is offering you.

You should try to use the full width of some of the easier runs and look for the often subtle changes in terrain. Use these rolls to help you unweight your skis — ride up the roll and then make a gentle turn on the top, so that you are completing the turn as you come down the back side. This will develop your ability to use all the available ingredients to

As you go over bumps and rolls, let your legs work with mountain. Do not push against it

make skiing easier, as well as subconsciously training you to use the bumps in the sort of style you'll need when you first step into a mogulfield.

You'll find it's fun exploring each piste you find yourself on — just keep an eye out for those parts of the piste which actively help you turn.

Looking forward

If you can see your ski tips when you are skiing you are not looking forward enough. If you concentrate on where your skis are going, you will only create more problems for yourself. This is because, by the time you try to react and make the corrections you need to make, it's probably too late. Your legs feed you all the information you need about where your skis are going, and you certainly find out quickly if they are misbehaving. If you concentrate on what is coming up ahead of you, you are more likely to be prepared for any changes or compensations you need to make on your descent. Additionally, you will be more aware of other

Always look ahead to see where you are going and see what lies in front. If you can see your ski tips then you are not looking far enough ahead

people around the slope — which is important from the point of view of safety — it gives you more chance of avoiding them!

Look ahead and you will notice more readily the changes in the snow conditions. You will also stand easier on your skis so that, if the skiing gets more difficult, you will be in a better frame of mind to handle the challenge. Also, being more aware of what is around you will have a comforting effect if you are finding the whole environment just a little bit hostile!

Pile on the calories!

Food, glorious food! As you are expending so much energy in the mountains, it is important to fuel up your tanks properly. It's not like going out to sit in the office for a few

hours, so your normal cup of coffee will simply not suffice. It's worth starting off with a good, wholesome breakfast — which you'll burn off quite easily over the next few hours. As you are exercising at altitude as well, your body needs to replenish liquid. The dry atmosphere depletes your normal reserves more quickly than you would imagine. If you are drinking a lot of coffee and alcohol, this will only aggravate the situation. Instead, drink a lot of other liquids during the day — a good big orange juice or mineral water at breakfast and the same at lunch. By drinking more non-alcoholic liquids, you will feel better and stronger over the course of the day and hence enjoy it all that bit more.

CHAPTER TWELVE

Skiing on ice

The word 'ice' strikes fear into the hearts of most skiers — but I must admit that I revel in the challenge of skiing on really hard snow. It's a very satisfying achievement to get the skis to behave when they are struggling for grip.

Most skiers have problems when they encounter patches of ice on a run because they try to do something different to get some grip and stop sliding around.

The best thing you can do under those circumstances is to be patient and to hold your position while you slide over the

Skiing on ice is like driving a car on snow

The best way to help your skiing on ice is to ensure that your skis are up to it by being well tuned

patch of ice — then you will be standing in the correct position to continue skiing normally when your skis grip again.

Skiing on ice for most skiers, is like driving a car on snow. If you hit the brakes in a car on a slippery surface, the chances are that you will spin off the road. Apply pressure gently and you will stop, slowly but surely, as the tyres find that little bit of grip which is available. The same thing goes with turning the steering wheel — sudden movements just create an initial skid, while gentle movements maintain the equilibrium of the car.

When you are skiing, don't try to rush your movements when you hit the dreaded ice. You might not feel in control, but if you make a sudden movement you will definitely be out of control — and more than likely, upside down!

There is not an awful lot you can do when you hit the ice, especially if you are not prepared for it — so don't do anything. That way you will probably have less of a problem.

If you are finding the runs quite icy, for example in the morning before the sun has had a chance to take the bite off the night frost, the best way to help your skiing is to ensure that your skis are up to it.

Skis for ice

Racers who battle down 'boiler-plate' icy courses have sharp edges that you could cut your fingers on, as well as using skis specially constructed to grip on this hard snow. Holiday skiers who have good skis with the correct performance for their ability, regularly serviced and in good condition, will frequently find that, when other members in the class are struggling, they will be cutting across the ice as if it wasn't there.

If your skis have seen years of thrashing down rocky pistes and your edges are dull, then even if you were Marc Girardelli, you would still have problems making short swings down a steep, icy slope. Certainly tackling ice, the workman has to look to his tools — and if they fail him, he's justified in blaming them!

To get a grip on a steep icy slope, assuming the skis are in good order, it is essential to get the basic technique right. Ice will amplify any bad habits or weaknesses in your skiing ability. The real key to skiing on ice is to be positive, and to take command of the situation. If you are apprehensive you don't have a chance. The only way to get the ski to grip is to have all your body-weight on the lower ski. Any weight on the upper ski will cause skidding, which will ultimately mean, nine times out of ten, that you will get more weight on the up-hill ski and slide out of the turn on your posterior.

You have to have your upper body well over the lower ski to get all your weight on this ski, and unless you are committed to the slope at this stage, you will find yourself struggling to get into this fairly aggressive stance, in what always feels to be a sticky situation.

In this position you will be able to exaggerate the edge set by having your knee angled well into the hill.

Precision is vital so that the pressure generated by your body-weight and amplified by centrifugal forces, can be applied in full only when the leading section of the ski edge has found an initial grip (especially for long turns). If you apply the pressure on the ski too quickly, the ski will skid initially until it finds more bite. This is why the top skiers have to be extremely sensitive and have tremendous feeling to be able to optimize the use of their strength on an icy course.

Remember, skiing on ice is about feeling — not brute strength, and to have that feeling you have to be able to relax. Confidence in yourself, and a positive approach to the tough and often terrifying ice, will see you conquer the toughest of snow conditions — but you do have to have the right tools for the job beneath your feet.

Regularly sharpening your edges will help you control your skis in difficult conditions

CHAPTER THIRTEEN

Skiing the moguls

It's very rare that you see a skier's face break into a smile when you watch them looking down a mogul field. There is always a handful of skiers who *do* enjoy the extra exertion that the vicious bumps demand of the body as they twist and wind their way through the seemingly never-ending maze of worn snow — but most holiday skiers just find moguls hard work.

The key to skiing moguls is to follow an imaginary route through the maze. Before you push off into the bumps, imagine that you are water in a mountain river. The river is just like the ones you see the white-water canoes racing down, with white water building up around the boulders and rocks strewn across it. Those boulders and rocks are very similar to the bumps in front of you. The water always finds the most direct — and subsequently the smoothest — path around the rocks.

Focus your attention

This is what you have to do. Think of the water flowing between the bumps in front of you, and focus your attention on the path the water would take. This should be your route down the slope, turning in the troughs between the bumps, trying to complete the turn before you hit the next one. The secret to this is not to think about finishing your turn in time —forget that part of the manoeuvre and just concentrate on making the next turn as soon as possible. Naturally, if you worry about making another turn, you will automatically finish the first turn in time.

If you think of yourself as the water, you will find that you turn more quickly down the fall-line, which is the way the water would flow, and then it is much easier to find a rhythm through the imaginary boulders. Practise this where the moguls are spaced out a bit, for instance on a more gentle slope, and you will find that you can literally 'flow' like a river.

To negotiate the bumps smoothly, you must always approach moguls a lot more slowly. Similarly, if you find yourself going too fast, then the best way to slow down is to turn more quickly, or to turn more across the hill. If you find yourself losing the rhythm, then you might have to absorb one bump, your knees going right up to your chest, to catch a trough again.

If you watch a good skier go through moguls, their head and chest will be almost stationary, while all the movement is really coming from the waist down, the legs extending and compressing to absorb the size of the mounds of snow that have been etched out by previous skiers.

When you tackle a mogul field, think of water flowing down through a mountain river. You should follow the route the water would around the large rocks

CHAPTER FOURTEEN

Powder snow

Powder skiing is to skiers what Shergar is to a jockey, or a Ferrari is to a driver — the ultimate. The beauty of virgin snow, fresh and deep, is an experience for which it is difficult to find a parallel anywhere else. Being able to master this, the ultimate of snow conditions, is perhaps one of the greatest rewards the sport can give you.

The frustration builds up, though, as you struggle through those first days. The temptingly light, soft snow draws you further into it, but makes it very awkward to collect yourself after each fall — and initially they occur with monotonous regularity.

The most common piece of advice that is handed around is 'lean back'. First-time powder skiers have visions of water-skiers behind speed boats — and they still end up falling over.

Learning the technique

To learn to ski in fresh snow, find a gentle slope with, ideally, between six inches and a foot of snow. Even if you were to go straight down this slope, you don't want to accelerate too quickly. Stop at the top of the slope and point your skis straight down the hill. You want to do linked turned from this point on, making sure you don't traverse between turns. Go straight from one turn to the next, keeping your skis a bit closer together than you might on the piste. Make sure the first turn is just a small one, and the next one is only a little bit bigger, and the next and so on.

Don't look at your skis — you probably won't be able to see them anyway (they will be under the snow with just the tips breaking the surface) and, as you should not be changing any of the rules from piste-skiing, you should not be looking at your skis off-piste either.

You must make sure that you are turning your skis by unweighting, so you keep the rhythm going from one turn to the next. Up-down-up-down-up-down — keep the rhythm going, and as along as you keep in the fall-line, you should slide down the hill quite effortlessly.

If you watch good skiers cutting beautiful tracks down

In powder snow the position of your skis relative to the slope will change, as the ski tips float out of the soft snow; your centre of gravity will adjust naturally to this when you move

untouched slopes, you will notice that all the tracks are linked turns down the fall line, except when they are traversing for access.

I am sure you will probably find the first step surprisingly easy, but then when you venture on to steeper terrain, you'll spend most of your time brushing the snow off your clothes. This is because you have moved on a step too quickly and are, in fact, making your life very difficult in the powder. The easy way down is to keep a rhythm in the fall-line. This applies to both the steep and the flat slopes — except on the steep ones, where you have to have more confidence, and the turn will have to be more exaggerated to control the speed.

The first time you move to the steeper slopes, you won't have the confidence to remain in the fall-line long enough to build up a rhythm. It is a lot easier to ski well in powder than it is to ski badly, because if you are cautious about letting the skis remain in the fall-line, you will want to have small traverses between the turns — and that's when the trouble starts. The bigger the turn out of the fall-line, the greater the likelihood of trouble. Rather than thinking about the next turn, just do it — 95% of the time it will work out. What about the other 5%? Well, powder snow is very soft.

When it comes to your weight distribution, you just need to keep BALANCED, over the centre of your skis, as you learned before. You will naturally find the position for your centre of gravity which is most suitable.

CHAPTER FIFTEEN

Steep slopes

As you peer down a steep slope, the process which works against you goes into action.

The problem with skiing down a steep slope is that you perceive the difficulties, as opposed to the steepness actually creating them for you. The vision of sliding uncontrollably down the mountain colours the nervous skier's imagination, ringing alarm bells all over his body.

Immediately the muscles get tense, and the co-ordination flies out of the window — no wonder you struggle as you go down the slope. You would be having problems if you were in similar shape on a piece of perfectly flat terrain!

Conquering vertigo

It's your anxiety which is creating your biggest problem. Standing at the top of a steep black run for the first time can make anyone nervous, especially if you have not spent much time in an alpine environment before. If you don't have confidence in yourself on skis, this will compound the vertigo even further, so the best advice is not to go tackling slopes which are really beyond your ability. All you will do is knock your confidence down a level which, in turn, makes your skiing regress another step.

Only move on to the tougher slopes when you feel fully confident on the easier terrain. You can still enjoy yourself sliding around the red runs — the mountains are not any more beautiful on a black run — in fact, if you bite off more than you can chew, they take on a distinctly sinister aspect!

Think positive

When you do feel confident enough to tackle the tougher slopes, the key to handling the change in pitch is to be more positive. You need to make all your turns more deliberate — and also quicker. Similarly, your weight transfer from one leg to the other should also be more pronounced in order to get extra grip with your edges.

Being positive will mean that you get your upper body

over the skis more, which naturally compensates for the fact that the slope is sliding away more quickly. This in turn means you can get more weight over the skis to give you more grip and control.

If you think that you have to do a lot of things differently, just because the slope looks a lot tougher, you only end up confusing yourself. Rely on what you have learnt so far, just be more positive and committed, and you will find yourself getting down those steep slopes so much more easily. This is because, if you have the basic foundations of your skiing ability correct, you can naturally adapt to the changes down a mountainside — just as long as your mind doesn't interfere!

On steep slopes rely on what you have learnt so far, just be more positive and committed and you will find the tougher slopes that much easier

CHAPTER SIXTEEN

Flat light

Talk of skiing always conjures up visions of a crisp, deep-blue sky and glistening white mountains — but on so many days of your holiday you will find yourself wrapped up in the cotton wool of the clouds which create the snow. Skiing either in cloud or a heavy snowfall is certainly a very different experience from racing across slopes in bright sunshine.

The bumps, seemingly invisible against the white background, always jump out at you when you least expect it and then, when the fog is really dense, you can hardly tell if you are moving at all.

Coping with bad visibility

When visibility is that bad, the first thing is to make sure that you have your bearings and know where you are on the mountain. Also keep an eye on the time, as you will have to ski more slowly in these conditions, and it will take you a bit longer to get down to the bottom.

Ideally you should ski with someone who knows the area like the back of their hand, for example, one of the local instructors — but if you have suddenly been engulfed by low cloud, this is not always possible. Flat light, snow fall or low cloud all pose the same problems. It is nearly impossible to gauge distances or pitches on the slopes, and if you have no references, this can totally disorientate you, radically affecting your balance.

Finding a reference

To give your mind a positive co-ordination point you must always have a vertical reference in sight. Ideally this could be the piste signs which should be — but aren't always — spaced evenly down the slope. This is the best way to find your way down the mountain, using as a cross-reference your piste map which, being an organized and safe skier, you have just plucked from your back pocket.

It is vital that you always have a vertical reference in your vision, as this will let you know if you are standing up or not, and if you are moving or not. That may sound funny, but in a complete white-out, you can fall over because you think you are moving when you have, in fact, stopped. If you can see a piste marker or a lift pylon, you have a reference point to help you make spatial judgements.

Naturally you will have to ski a lot more slowly because you cannot see very well (but that is the same if you are

In flat light develop all your senses, feel the snow and listen carefully. Try to pick up a vertical reference in your vision to help co-ordinate your balance

driving a car in foggy conditions) and perhaps you need to adapt your style to suit your reduced speed. If you need to go really slowly, the safest way down is to spread your skis out into a good, stable snowplough position.

Sharpen up your senses

Blind people develop their other senses to compensate for their lack of vision, and the same applies to skiers in really bad visibility. Listen and feel very carefully what is happening around you. If you feel the snow conditions below you and the changes which are continuously taking place, this will help you prepare your legs for any larger bumps which come up. Similarly, you can feel when you have better snow below you, particularly if the conditions are changing (typical when snow is falling heavily), so that you can make a turn where the snow feels smoother and where you are less likely to catch an edge.

Listening is also important to help you keep your bearings. Try to hear ski lifts nearby — these immediately give you a good indication of where you are — and remember to listen out for other skiers in the area.

By concentrating your three senses, sight, hearing and feeling, on the stark conditions, you will be focussing your mind to such an extent that, as long as you are skiing slowly, you can relax your body and be loose and supple enough to react to the surprises the mountain will throw at you from the secrecy of all that frustrating cloud.

CHAPTER SEVENTEEN

Falling

Falling is an important part of skiing — basically because everyone does it! If you remember that, without exception, all skiers fall over, then perhaps when you find yourself in a pile, covered in snow, you won't feel so self-conscious about it.

There are different ways of falling, and it pays to try to fall the easier way! If you fight the fall too much you often find yourself more likely to get injured. The fighting often

Do not "fight" a fall, everyone falls over! Try and fall over the easier way — make sure your most padded parts hit the deck first

comes from in-built vanity — that feeling that 'biting the dust' is a reflection of your lack of ability.

If you feel your are going over, then let yourself go the way that gravity is pulling you — just try to make sure your most padded part hits the deck first if possible. Similarly, if you feel that you are getting out of control, just sit back and on to the hill. Suddenly you will be sitting comfortably in the snow — definitely the lesser of two evils. As you've probably gathered, the other alternative is racing down the slope out of control — and then you might hit something a bit harder!

When you have fallen, the first thing you should do is get your skis across the hill and below you. To get back up, there are many different ways, and quite simply the best way is the one which you find the most convenient.

CHAPTER EIGHTEEN

Getting ready to ski

When you get out of your car or off the bus in the ski resort, you should be all ready to go and enjoy yourself. You've left behind the constraints of life at home and work — and the last thing you need now is the worry of queuing up to get skis, boots, photographs for lift passes and foreign currency. If you are prepared before you go away, your chances of having a trouble-free holiday are greatly improved.

The process which takes the longest, however, is rearranging your muscles to take the shock of the exertion they will be going through on the slopes.

Even when I was racing and doing physical training six hours a day, when I first stepped on to skis, I still found muscles that I thought didn't exist. Skiing has a great knack of exploring the complete human anatomy. Getting your body ready for skiing doesn't mean that for two months prior to hitting the slopes you should don a track-suit and become a closet athlete — but it does help to improve your physical condition slightly. Skiing is a good excuse to trim yourself up. No doubt, the benefits will be obvious at work too, as your concentration level improves. The motivation of the skiing holiday is already having positive effects.

The best way to do any training is to do what you enjoy doing — that way it is a lot easier to do more and work a bit harder. So, if you are not particularly sporty and, for example, enjoy your shopping, make sure that you avoid using lifts and escalators and stretch out as you go up the steps. Eventually try to go up two steps at a time. Get off the bus or tube one stop early and have a good walk. If you do this for two months before you go up to the mountains, you will feel much better on your first day on skis.

What you will achieve is an improvement in your basic level of fitness, which will be really noticeable — and that will give you an extra ounce of confidence which can have only positive effects.

If you play squash or tennis, attempt to play more frequently and throw in the occasional jog or bike ride. Cycling is an effective way to improve your basic condition for skiing, so if you were to ride to work a couple of times a week, this would help trim you up.

The main thing with getting your body into shape is that,

The best way to improve your fitness before you ski is to do a bit more of the sport you enjoy most

whatever you do — and as you can see, these small things can all add up to help you — you must do them consistently.

The reason that I do not recommend a complete exercise programme is that, for many people, the enthusiasm wanes quite quickly, so that after a few hot and sweaty muscle-torturing sessions, the novelty wears off and frequently so does the enthusiasm. If you continually make small additions of exercise to your daily routine you will gradually improve your physical condition.

For those who feel that they need to make a big step forward by greatly improving their fitness, then the popular aerobics or dance classes are an excellent and enjoyable way of taking your fitness factor up a few notches.

A good game of soccer or rugby, played twice a week will also improve the general condition for those who enjoy team games and, surprisingly, horse-riders always seem to handle the sport on two planks with remarkable ease. So, if riding is your sport, make sure you can get in some good rides before you head off to the mountains.

When you are working on your body, it's a good idea to organize all the bits and pieces that make life easier on the snow. A good weather-proof jacket and salopettes or ski jeans are essential, plus you need a selection of shirts and pullovers. I use normal T-shirts as vests — the modern ones are usually quite long, which is important for keeping your back warm. This is an area of the body which takes a lot of stress, and if you keep it warm it will stay in better shape.

A selection of roll-neck shirts — preferably with zips or buttons so that you can regulate the internal temperature a bit — is useful to wear under the sweater, which I prefer to be thinner, as I find thick jumpers too bulky and restrictive under a ski jacket.

If squash or tennis is your game, play more frequently before your skiing holiday

If you are out shopping, use the stairs, instead of the escalators and try to take two steps at a time.

The advantage, too, with wearing normal sweaters or sweatshirts is that you most probably have a cupboard full of them, so you don't need to buy anything extra. Remember too, that if it gets really cold, it is more effective to wear two thin pullovers than one thick one.

Under the salopettes you can wear long-johns, or I use a pair of track-suit bottoms if it is cold. Again, this is easier, as you just take off the salopettes and you are ready and comfortable for a relaxing tea. It's worth having two pairs of gloves — one as a spare in case your main pair don't dry quickly enough for the next day's skiing. If you get cold hands, buy a pair of mittens, as these tend to keep your hands warmer.

Sports glasses and goggles are worth getting in advance so that you are sure that the ones you buy will protect your eyes. The sun is one hundred times stronger at altitude than it is at home, and glasses designed for skiing should have a total UV block to screen your eyes from harmful rays. Children especially should have good sunglasses, so always ask to see if they have protective lenses — just because lenses are dark, it doesn't mean they will reduce the strength of dangerous rays effectively.

Good ski goggles are also helpful in improving visibility when it's snowing, and they are designed not to mist up — but they cannot perform miracles if they are covered in snow.

The best way to look after goggles is to wear them only when you are actually skiing. Keep them dry in an inside pocket before you get out on to the slopes then, when you are ready to ski off, brush any loose snow from the top of your hat or hair and take the goggles out, keeping the outside of the lens up so that snow can't fall on the inside. Lift the lens straight up to your face and pull the strap over your head. If you pull the strap over your head with the goggles on your hat, they will collect all the snow from the top of your head. Ideally, the inside of the goggles should always remain dry. When you get to the bottom of the run, pull the strap over your head and take the goggles off your face to return them to the safety of your pocket.

When you stop for lunch, make sure you put them somewhere safe and dry — if you have bought a good pair, they will have a cloth with which to dry off excess moisture without damaging the lens.

Don't forget to protect your skin against the strength of the alpine sun. Make sure you have enough cream with you, and for children in particular, take a good sun block. It isn't just that the sun works hard on your face — the wind and cold can also be very harsh. Protective sun creams help keep your skin moist and supple and will reduce the strong burning rays which, you should remember, also penetrate cloud and fog.

Take ski socks with you which are long enough to come up to your knee — and I recommend that you wear just the one pair of long socks. They shouldn't be too thick, or they will reduce the support which your ski boots give you.

Small things, such as having a passport photograph ready for your lift pass, having a selection of sticking plasters and so on, may seem trivial — but mostly you'll find you only need them when you haven't got any!

Finally, keep a check list so that you are sure everything you need is packed safely before you set out on your travels.

CHAPTER NINETEEN

Equipment pointers

Part of getting ready for your holiday should be ensuring that your equipment is properly organized.

If you have skied a couple of times, it is certainly worth having a complete set of equipment. The value of having your own ski boots is painfully obvious after you have suffered the agony to which ill-fitting boots can subject you. The advantages of having your own skis are not as immediate, although many people see this as being just as important.

Although a bad workman should not blame his tools, if your skis are not maintained regularly and serviced, your chances of having much control when the snow gets a bit icy are greatly reduced. Even on a smooth piste, a good, well-prepared pair of skis will turn a lot more smoothly and easily than skis which have suffered weeks of wear and tear.

Your own skis

If you have your own skis, when you arrive in the resort you know that you are ready to go skiing, and you can avoid the queue in the rental shop.

Your bindings will be up-to-date and be adjusted exactly to your weight and ability, so that you know that the safety aspect has been properly taken care of. You can choose the system which is the most convenient to use or the easiest to handle.

Skis are now designed to suit each different standard of skier, so you can get a model which will suit your style and will make your life as easy as possible on the slopes. Ideally you should choose a pair of skis as long as possible for your height and ability. Just because they are shorter, doesn't mean they will be any easier to turn. If you ski a bit faster, short skis will be too unstable, and it is the stability of your skis which gives you the confidence to initiate good turns. Naturally if you don't ski so well or as frequently, you might well choose a shorter ski.

Each future holiday you go on, the first time you get on to your skis, you will know what they are going to do for you — that's one more variable out of the window!

Boots

Choosing a pair of ski boots can be a tricky procedure. You need to get a pair which are really comfortable — and often after a few days that initial comfort fades away and the pain creeps in. One of the reasons is that, when you buy boots you forget that a ski boot needs to hold your foot quite firmly — so you end up buying a pair which are too big. Always choose boots as small as possible — they're OK just as long as you can wriggle your toes.

Ski boots should fit snugly, just like a pair of new tennis shoes. After a day or two, the boot will get used to your foot and vice versa — then you should have a perfect fit. If you don't have a snug fit initially, you will end up with too much space. It's important to buy a pair you feel comfortable in — friend's recommendations might not always be suitable for you, as feet vary considerably.

There are two basic types of ski boot on the market — rear-entry and front-entry. The difference is that the rear-entry boot tends to be more convenient, but front-entry boots give you a little bit more support and control as the shell closes more tightly to your foot. The days of skiers having to suffer on the slopes are long gone. It should be possible to get comfortable boots for even the strangest of feet.

Ski boots should fit like a pair of running or tennis shoes. Wearing ski boots around the house before your holiday will help you get used to them

Equipment care

Ski equipment is a serious investment which can really contribute to your enjoyment on holiday — but to protect this investment, you can extend the life of your gear by looking after it all carefully. The skis and bindings should be serviced regularly, just like a car. If you are on a two-week holiday, it's worth taking the skis to the local shop for a 'wax and tune' to keep the edges sharp, while at the end of your holiday you should take the skis back to your local ski shop at home and have the bases waxed and repaired and the edges tuned up again before you store them away. Remember too, to take the skis out of the ski bag when you stow them away — ski bags don't breathe, and if there's a little water from melted snow left, this will accelerate corrosion on your metal edges.

If you've done all these things, you should be ready to go next winter. Just remember, if your skiing improves dramatically, or you gain or lose a bit of weight, your ski bindings might need readjusting. Do this by taking your skis to a recognized dealer — their staff are trained to do the job properly.

You need to treat your ski boots as if they were a good pair of shoes. Don't just chuck them off your feet at the end of the day and leave them in a corner on the floor of your

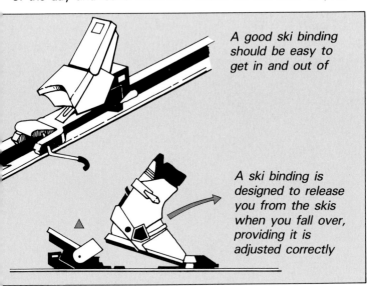

A good ski binding should be easy to get in and out of

A ski binding is designed to release you from the skis when you fall over, providing it is adjusted correctly

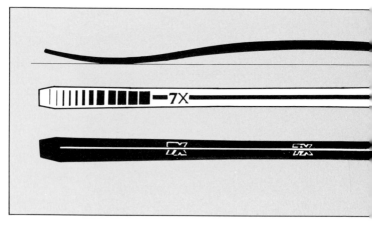

hotel. Make sure they are near a radiator and are tidily stacked away with the tongues neatly pushed back into the boot. You can't expect your boots to be comfortable if you don't look after the insides.

Let your boots dry out overnight, as your feet perspire quite a lot, even if it is cold. There is always a lot of humidity absorbed by the liner which needs to be dried out

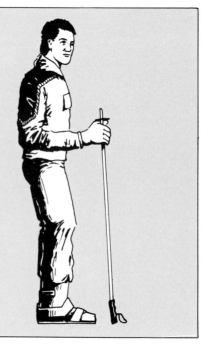

The correct length for a ski pole. Just turn the pole upside down, with the hand below the basket and make sure your forearm is level

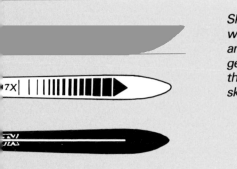

Skis are designed with different flexes and different geometries to suit the varying needs of skiers.

before the next day's skiing — or you'll start the day with cold, wet feet.

Most inner liners come out of the boots and, particularly if it is cold, it is a good idea to take these out of the plastic shells to ensure that they have every chance to dry out — you'll be surprised how warm they are the next day.

When you get back from your holiday, take the boots out of their carrying bag. They are sure to have quite a bit of moisture in them, so you should make sure they are properly dried out before you store them away. Watch out too, if you know you have mice around — they love the toe end of ski boots and this can have far-reaching effects on your comfort the next time around!

Just to reassure yourself, it's worth trying on your boots at home before you leave on holiday — just to make sure they still fit. If you find they're not so good, go back to the shop where you bought them and they will be able to make some small adjustments to get that fit back again.

CHAPTER TWENTY

Summary – the last run

By the time you have read this far in my book, you will have seen that there are many different small points one can remember. Ultimately when you are out on the slopes the easiest way to maintain a progression in your learning curve is not to do too much at one time.

Each day, just try one of seeds of thought that I am attempting to sow, and repeat it until it becomes a matter of course. If you try too many things at a time, then they do not become instinctive.

This is why it takes TIME to learn to ski. I remember when I was learning, I would compare the films my parents took of me to see how much I had learned on the last holiday. I used to get really excited when my feet would shift, a few inches, closer together. That was the style then! So my progress was slow and gentle, but it gave me a good base to work from.

It is also important to realise the significance of just improving one item of your performance at a time on the slope. Try to avoid changing too much of your natural performance at one time, otherwise if you change a few things you do not know which of the changes made the improvement.

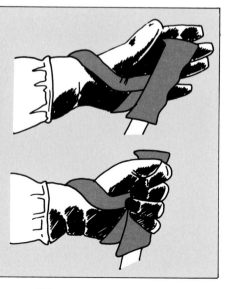

Gripping your ski poles. Put your hand upwards through the strap so it is looped round the wrist. Now grip the pole handle with the strap between your thumb and forefinger

If you find the right "key" then suddenly you will find yourself doing things on the mountains you really thought you never would.

It's trying to find the "key" that makes the sport so much fun and interesting.

One important fact to remember is that if you like travelling to different resorts you will need a bit of time to adjust to the new environment. Skiing is no different than golf, as it is extemely rare that you will hit your best score on a new course. So give yourself a bit of time to adjust to any new resort. Unfortunately there is no substitute for time, coupled with patience, on the snow, so there is a good reason to go back to the slopes again and again, and enjoy the spectacular mountains.

Index